KNOWABOUT

Sorting

KNOWABOUT Sorting

Text: Henry Pluckrose
Photography: Chris Fairclough

Franklin Watts

London/New York/Sydney/Toronto

© 1988 Franklin Watts

First published in the USA by

Franklin Watts Inc
387 Park Avenue South
New York 10016

ISBN: 0–531–10548–2
Library of Congress
Catalog Card No: 87–51711

Editor: Ruth Thomson
Design: Edward Kinsey

Typesetting: Keyspools Limited
Printed in Hong Kong

About this book

This book is designed for use in the home, play group, and preschool.

Mathematics is part of the child's world. It is not just about interpreting numbers or mastering the tricks of addition or multiplication. Mathematics is about ideas. These ideas (or concepts) have been developed over the centuries to help explain particular qualities, such as size, weight, height, as well as relationships and comparisons. Yet all too often the important part which an understanding of mathematics will play in a child's development is forgotten or ignored.

Most adults can solve simple mathematical tasks by "doing them in their head." For example, you can probably add up or subtract simple numbers without the need for counters, beads or fingers. Young children find such abstractions almost impossible to master. They need to see, talk, touch and experiment.

The photographs in this book and the text that supports them have been prepared with one major aim. They have been chosen to encourage talk around topics that are essentially mathematical. By talking with you, the young reader will be helped in exploring some of the central concepts that emphasize mathematics. It is upon an understanding of these concepts that a child's future mastery of mathematics will be built.

What a mess!
How could you sort it out?

There are some animals . . .

some buttons . . .

four cars . . .

and six pencils.

Look how the animals have been sorted.

Why have they been grouped like this?

The pencils have been sorted
in a special way too.

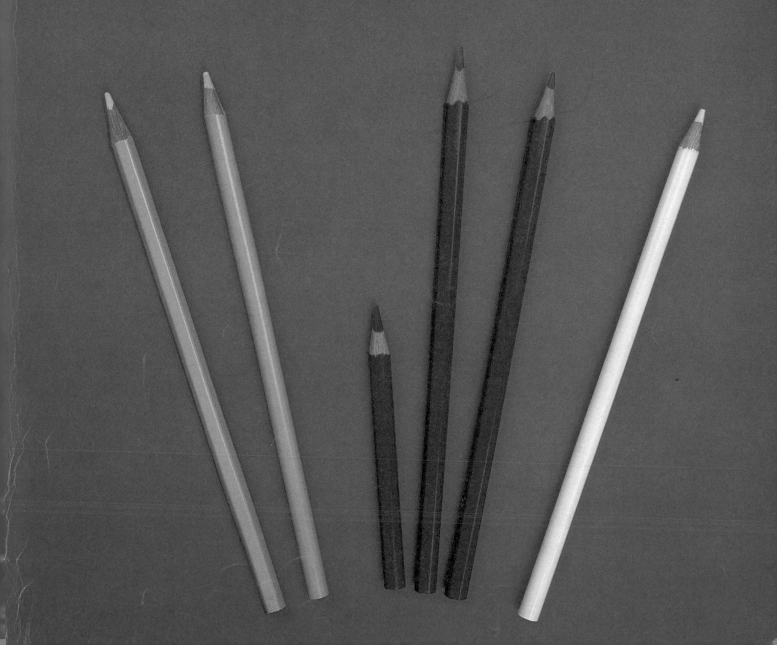

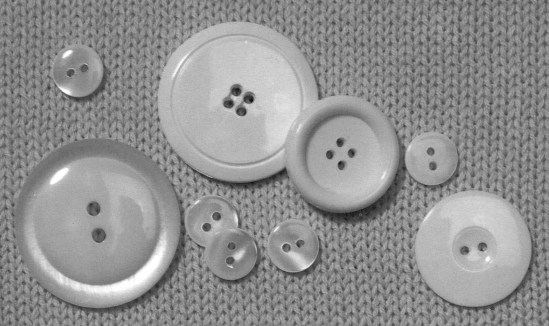

The buttons could be sorted
like this . . .

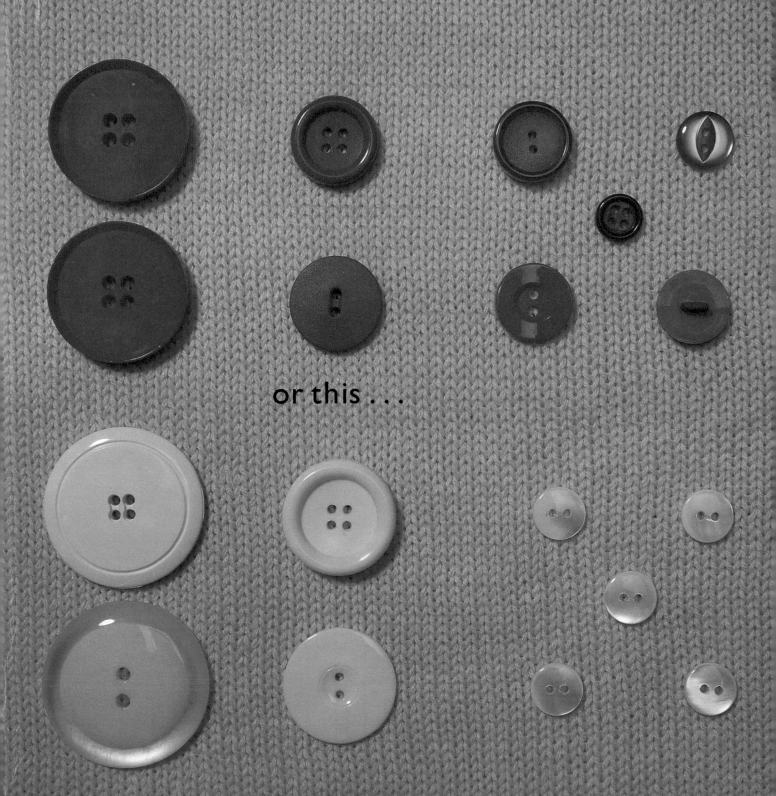

or this . . .

or even
like this.

All the red things
could be put together
like this.

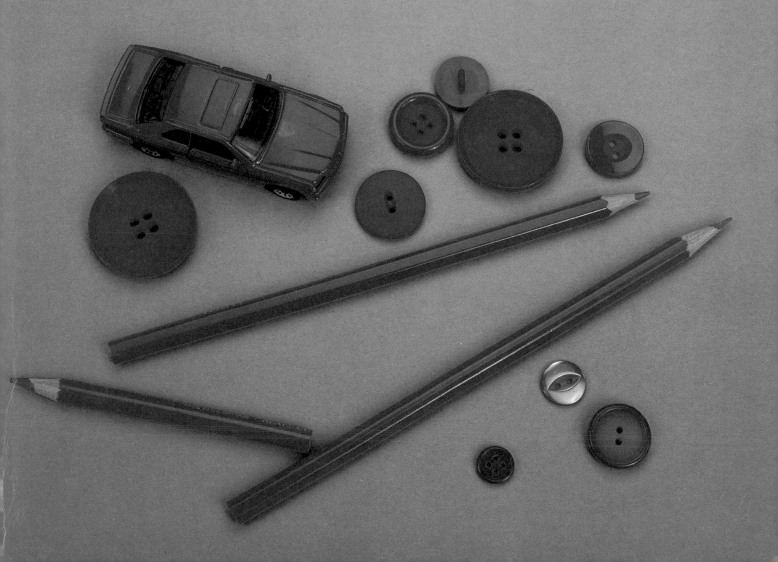

How could you sort
these flowers?

How could you sort
these shoes?

This is a set
of playing cards.

This is a set
of dishes.

What does a set mean?

Setting
is another word
for sorting.

These are plant seeds.

It helps gardeners
if the seeds are sorted
before they are sold.

You put things
into sets,
when you put away
knives and forks . . .

or when you set the table.

Shopkeepers arrange their displays in sets.

Why won't you find any fruit here?

Is this a set?

Is this a set?

Make a pile of your own things.
See how many different ways
you can sort it.